WILL
POWER

Lynda Field

VERMILION

LONDON

First published in 1999 by Element Books.

This edition published in 2000 by Vermilion, an imprint of Ebury Press,
Random House, 20 Vauxhall Bridge Road, London SW1V 2SA

www.randomhouse.co.uk

Random House Australia (Pty) Limited
20 Alfred Street, Milsons Point, Sydney, New South Wales 2061, Australia

Random House New Zealand Limited
18 Poland Road, Glenfield, Auckland 10, New Zealand

Random House South Africa (Pty) Limited
Endulini, 5A Jubilee Road, Parktown 2193, South Africa

The Random House Group Limited Reg. No. 954009

Papers used by Vermilion are natural, recyclable products made from
wood grown in sustainable forests.

Printed and bound in Denmark by Nørhaven A/S, Viborg

A CIP catalogue record for this book is available from the British Library

ISBN 0-09-185729-5

Dedicated to
my husband, Richard,
whose Man Power I love.

Introduction

Woman power is the power that all women share as a birthright. It is the power that enables us to use the unique and amazing gifts of womanhood, to be creative and flexible; to overcome obstacles with humour and perseverance; to have endurance and patience; to love and appreciate ourselves and all those around us; to reach our potential; to reach for the stars; to live our dreams.

Woman Power is your power –
embrace it!

Create New Boundary Lines

Women are very good at giving away their time, energy, creativity and love. Well, everyone seems to need us, don't they? No wonder we sometimes want to shout, 'What about me?' Well, shout it! Then take action.

When someone next asks you a favour, don't automatically agree to it.

Assess your true feelings. If you say 'yes' but experience fear, anger, intimidation, resentment, irritation or low self-esteem it's time to create a new boundary line. Say to yourself, 'I will go this far and no further.' You can be a good friend / partner / mother / daughter / workmate and still say 'no'.

Become Attractive

*'The only way to have a friend
is to be one.'*
Ralph Waldo Emerson

Become the friend you would like
most to have. If you want to be
popular and attract new people into
your life, you need to use the
following skills.

* Expand your interests and your
  network will grow.

* Listen well. People feel valued when they have your undivided attention.

* Empathize, show that you understand.

* Develop your small-talk skills; find out what interests the other person. Light-hearted talk relaxes people.

Become known as someone who is non-threatening and supportive, and you will attract new relationships.

Say Positive Things about Yourself

Do you ever say things like:

'I'm no good; I can't do that; trust me to mess up?'

When you speak negatively about yourself others will soon start to agree with you. Great opportunities will pass you by: who wants to give that super job to someone who always messes up? The more you bring yourself down, the lower your confidence levels fall.

Speak positively about yourself. Say things like: 'I'm getting better at ...; I'll give it my best shot; I always learn from my mistakes!' Be positive, feel confident and see how others respond.

See the Beauty

Many times I have driven through the most amazing countryside, so preoccupied with my thoughts that I have arrived having missed it all. Sometimes our lives can become so sterilized and automatic: driving from centrally-heated houses to centrally-heated / air conditioned offices ... who knows what the weather is like and who cares?

As we lose touch with the natural world we lose our sense of belonging to something larger than ourselves, so the wonder and excitement of our lives fade away.

Today, wherever you are, go out into the world and focus consciously on the beauty which surrounds you. Feel connected.

Trust Your Intuition

Women have a much more highly developed intuitive faculty than men but we don't always trust our hunches, flashes of insight or feeling of knowingness. We have been taught the value of logic and how to 'reason things out' but, as we know, our rational minds cannot always provide all the answers.

Think of a difficult situation in your life. Close your eyes, relax and ask

your intuition to help you to resolve
the problem. Repeat this process over
the next few days. New insights will
come forward (in any shape or form,
at any time – be prepared).
Act on them!

Speak Well of Others

When we speak badly about other people we also change the way we feel about ourselves. How do you feel about a person who gossips about others? Could you trust such a person? Could they be a good friend to you?

Next time you find yourself speaking badly about someone, notice what you are doing. Do you need to say these things? Will it change anything for the better? If it won't, then stop.

Always look for something positive to say about other people and you will find that you will all feel better about yourselves.

State Your Needs

How often do you get what you
really want?

Many women tell me that they fall
short of their desires, life treats them
badly and people let them down. If
this sounds like you, check your
communication techniques.

Examples:

So he didn't take you out on your
birthday.

Question: Did you ask him to?

You were left with all the clearing up after the party.

Question: Did you ask for help? Did you refuse help?

You don't feel like cooking the dinner (again!) but you do it (resentfully).

Question: Did you tell anyone how you felt?

Enjoy a One-minute Face-lift

Use this pressure-point massage technique to stimulate the circulation to your skin, energize your facial tissues and give your face an instant lift.

1. Press lightly with your fingertips between your eyes on either side of your nose. Move up to your eyebrows, pressing as you go.

2. Press along your eyebrows.

3. Apply pressure at the outside corner of your eyes.

4. Apply pressure at your temples.

5. Move to under your eyes, pressing your way down to the centre of your cheeks.

6. Press downwards towards your mouth, stopping at your gum-line. Press and move to the outside edges of your jaw and press again.

Let Go of Your Emotional Baggage

We carry around so many problems, worries and negative thoughts that we can often be weighed down by our emotional baggage.

Have you ever looked forward to an event only to find that on the day your pleasure is spoiled by the non-stop chatter of your worrying mind? Whenever you are feeling tense and worried, stop for a moment wherever you are and visualize yourself putting large suitcases of negative emotions down on to the ground. See yourself walking away from them.

Leave your worries behind you; they can wreck your life.

Make Today a Special Day

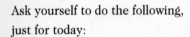

Ask yourself to do the following, just for today:

* Just for today I will encourage people and not criticize them.

* Just for today I will think positively.

* Just for today I will smile whenever I remember to.

* Just for today I will forgive myself.

* Just for today I will do three things I need to do but don't want to do.

* Just for today I will perform an act of kindness which will remain a secret.

* Just for today I will believe in myself.

* Just for today I will love my life.

Get Out of Addictive Relationships

You are in an addictive relationship if conversations, situations, emotions and thoughts keep repeating themselves, making you feel unhappy. Physical types might even recur in your life: you always go for muscular, dark men or blond, boyish types or ...

We cannot change, grow or fulfil our potential if we are stuck in addictive relationships, however, we justify them to ourselves: 'he treats me badly but I know he needs me so I must stay'; 'she's a good friend even though she always brings me down'. Break away from negative dependencies; go for friendships with totally different types of people.

You deserve supportive relationships.

Believe in Yourself

Henry Ford said,

'If you believe that you can do a thing, or if you believe you cannot, in either case you are right.'

And there you have it! You are what you believe you are, you will become what you expect to become – the choice is yours.

Little girls are often taught to take passive and receptive roles, and these grown-up little girls may find it hard to expect the best for themselves.

Increase your self-expectations – you can do / be / create more. Trust your judgement; believe in yourself.

Feel Like You're Falling in Love

Remember the last time you fell in love? How did you feel? Ecstatic, powerful, creative, amazing, in control ... and the world moved in harmony with you.

Wouldn't it be great to feel like that all the time? Well, you can but you need to concentrate on your relationship with yourself. Put yourself first for a while.

Take the energy you would spend on a new love and spend it on yourself.

* Appreciate yourself – mind, body and soul.
* Give yourself gifts.
* Take space and time to be alone.

Before we can love others, ecstatically and wholeheartedly, we need to learn to love ourselves.

Move On

So you didn't get the job / an important relationship has ended / you weren't invited to the party. And now you feel rejected, fed up, out of control, unloved ...

Feel the feelings and then move on. Don't let disappointment wreck your confidence and enthusiasm. No one has a clear pathway: life is all about meeting obstacles, overcoming them and moving on.

Keep focused on your goals and be ready to change your approach ('that job wasn't right for me'; 'it's time I lived on my own' ...). Success is all about keeping on keeping on. Bounce back from adversity and be ready to move on.

Let Your Creative Juices Flow

We are all creative, yet women often disagree: 'No, I'm not, I can't sing, draw, write; I'm tone deaf; can't paint, dance, sew ...' We can often trace these negative beliefs back to our childhood. Maybe a teacher told you that you couldn't sing, or someone laughed at your drawing. One small childhood incident can ruin a lifetime of creative skills.

Do you believe that you are non-creative? Try to think where this belief has come from and weed it out! Everything you do is creative; you are an artist creating your own environment, thoughts and relationships. Let your creative juices flow.

Keep Your Marriage Dynamic

It has often been said that a woman marries a man, thinking that she can and will change him, whereas the man thinks that the woman will be exactly the same forever. Small wonder that the divorce rate is so high!

Despite the difficulties, committed partnerships can flourish. Here are a

express your needs clearly? Can you say 'no'? Are you ready to take responsibility for your decisions and actions?

If there is nothing you can do to change your circumstances at work, you can always leave. However, amazing things can happen when you stop acting like a victim.

Recognize Your Believing Mirrors

✳

Who is it that tells you, 'Yes, you can do it'; 'I'll help you'; 'Go on, give it a go, there's nothing to lose' ...? List all the people in your life who encourage you and reflect your true potential. These people will be positive thinkers who are themselves well-focused and they will mirror back to you all your own possibilities.

We often spend time trying to make poor relationships work. Why not use that time instead to nurture your relationships with those who will support you?

Recognize your believing mirrors: they reflect your highest dreams.

Know Yourself

Who do you think you are?

Sometimes when we feel lacking in
confidence it is because we have
(temporarily) lost sight of our true
selves. We don't know what to think,
what to decide, even what to wear.
Perhaps we have been fulfilling other
people's wishes and needs.

Reclaim yourself. Find out where you are at and what makes you really tick by completing the following statements:

* I most enjoy ....
* My deepest desire is to ....
* If only I could ....
* My secret wish is ....
* My greatest regret is ....
* Tomorrow I will change the way I ....

Get Him to Talk it Over

You are having a row with the man in your life when suddenly he leaves to meet his mates / go to the pub / go for a drive ... and you are left high and dry, full of unresolved emotions.

How often has this happened to you? Scientific research shows that, whilst women automatically direct emotions to a part of the brain which enables them to talk about their feelings, men channel their emotions into actions rather than language (surprise surprise!).

Encourage him to express his feelings (he may need help with this) and your relationship will improve magnificently.

Ignore Your Inner Critic

We women find it so much easier
to be self-critical than to praise
ourselves. The part of us which nags
away and is never satisfied with our
performance (it could have been so
much better!) is called the 'Inner
Critic'.

If you are constantly bringing yourself
down in some way, look closely at

your beliefs. Are you really stupid / lazy / not good enough ...?

Ninety-nine point nine per cent of the time you will have been listening to your Inner Critic. Ignore its voice. You are an amazing woman!

Be Free

✳

As lovers / daughters / wives /
workers / mothers / grandmothers,
we can be pulled in so many
directions. Sometimes it feels as if we
are at the hub of a wheel, keeping all
the spokes in place so that the people
in our lives can function.

This feeling of being needed can limit
our creative flow and cut us off from

our own dreams and passions. How often have you not done something because it meant putting your own needs before someone else's?

See yourself standing tall, alone on the top of a mountain, and say, 'I am free to be me.' Repeat whenever necessary.

Assess your Compatibility Levels

Discover how compatible you will be with that new man / new girlfriend, by doing this assessment:

1. List six men and six women whom you have admired.

2. Think about why you like / love these people.

3. Next to each of their names list their positive characteristics,

e.g. confident, charming, bold, creative, thoughtful, spiritual, rational ...

4. Compare these lists and pull out those characteristics that your people all have in common. For example, you might discover that you are drawn to exciting, creative women and to supportive and successful men.

Use this information to assess your compatibility levels with the people who enter your life.

Be Courageous
for a Day

Do you ever catch yourself thinking or
saying, 'I'd love to … but I couldn't
possibly do it'? We have dreams and
desires that remain unfulfilled, not
because we tried and failed but
because we never tried at all.

What would you love to do and
haven't because you fear the risk of
failing, rejection or feeling a fool?

Take this day and live it courageously: say what you think, do what you want, take the risk. What is the worst thing that can happen to you? Let your courageous day become a courageous tomorrow. You can't possibly do it? Oh yes, you can!

Ground Yourself

Feeling jangled, tense, stretched or spaced out? Try grounding yourself.

Stand or sit with your feet apart, soles flat on the ground. Close your eyes and steady your breathing. Become aware of a point at the centre of the soles of both feet. These are the energy centres which connect you to the earth. Feel the energy, feel the connection. Some people imagine iron rods from their feet leading to the earth's centre, others visualize roots connecting them. Breathe slowly and feel the pull into the earth.

We are creatures of the earth but sometimes we forget where our true roots lie.

Discover Your
Inner Child

❋

Children have such a fresh way of seeing the world. They can be excited and amazed by things which may seem very ordinary to our grown-up eyes. Re-awaken the little girl within you and bring some wonder back into your life.

Re-create some favourite childhood experiences: go and eat a sherbet dip;

ride a donkey; sit on a hay bale; play with marbles; go to the fair and smell the candyfloss, and even eat it! ... As you bite that toffee apple you *are* the child within you.

Do at least one playful thing each day; the experience will grow on you.

Make a Love List

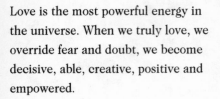

Love is the most powerful energy in the universe. When we truly love, we override fear and doubt, we become decisive, able, creative, positive and empowered.

So what do you love that can make you feel as good as this? Make a list of thirty things that you love. Be specific about them, for example: snowflakes falling in the dusk; the fourth track on a certain CD; the sound of your best friend's voice; knitting; Great Aunt Nell's chocolate fudge cake (hot with cream); the hairs on the back of your young son's neck ...

Love feelings will empower you. Write another list.

Respect Motherhood

✳

Being a mother is the most challenging / amazing / difficult / fascinating / frightening job I have ever done (and am still doing). I know that every mother reading this will also have experienced the emotional roller-coaster ride of motherhood. We go into uncharted territory (who knew it would be like this!) and we need to hang on to our hats (and our self-esteem).

Make a list of the following points and refer to it constantly:

* Motherhood is important.
* I don't have to feel guilty.
* There are no perfect mothers!
* I am doing my best.
* I can let go ...

Smile to Change
Your Life

It's a bad day; you are feeling
unhappy, sad, depressed ... You look
low and you can't communicate with
others, so the bad feelings increase.
Yet a smile can often break a negative
cycle of:

* feeling down
* looking dejected / being unable to
  communicate with others

* others stopping communicating with us

* enhanced feelings of depression ('you see, I'm so worthless no one wants to know me' ...)

SMILE! (Eyes as well!) Fake it until you make it (this really does work). The smiling habit can take you outside of yourself and help put it all back in perspective.

Send Light

Have you ever watched a disaster on TV and felt that there was nothing you could do? Have you heard that someone is ill or depressed but felt helpless in the face of their pain? Well, you can add your light to their life and lighten their load. Whenever you hear of suffering send a beam of white light – to a person, to a disaster, to a problem.

White light is a healing balm which brings enlightenment to the sender and the receiver. Don't analyze this process – just do it and feel what happens. Keep practising!

Manage Your Precious Time

Are you continually rushing hither and thither, trying to catch up with your life, juggling as you go? If your time is valuable to you, start to manage it.

1. Create lists of things to do – use a pinboard and a diary.

2. Look at the lists, pinboard and diary!

3. Prioritize your jobs. Delete those things that you don't really need to do.

4. Stop procrastinating – you will lose self-respect if you carry on.

5. Say 'no' when necessary and say it at once.

6. Enjoy the free time you have created. Don't just take on more work to fill in the gaps.

Remember that You Are Unique

Do you ever compare yourself with other people? Do you ever feel that you are 'not as good as' someone else, or not sufficiently clever / thin / beautiful / worthy / happy?

Every time you compare yourself with someone else you are behaving like a victim with low self-esteem. You are unique: There never has been, and there never will be, another person on this planet who is just like you. This makes you original and special.

Make this affirmation:

I am unique, original and special.

Say this over and over, sing it in the shower, in the car. Love your uniqueness.

Create a Firmer Bottom

Do this before you eat your breakfast
and again before you eat dinner. If you
make a habit of this little exercise,
you can expect a firmer bottom in a
few weeks.

1. Put a chair against a wall. Stand in
   front of it, extending both arms in
   front of you and keeping your
   head straight.

2. As you count to five lower yourself slowly into the chair, keeping your back straight, arms outstretched and keeping your chin level.

3. Count to five as you raise yourself back to the standing position.

The more you do this exercise, the quicker the results!

Welcome Silence

Faxes, car phones, TV, cell phones, e-mail – we're all so busy communicating our thoughts to other people. Our high velocity / voltage society encourages us to stay in touch with everyone except ourselves.

Turn off all communication appliances or find a place where you can't be contacted. Welcome some silence into your life.

Consciously seek silence for a few minutes each day: do nothing, just listen. Welcome silence and you will hear your own inner voice. Listen with your heart and stay in touch with your deepest needs.

Go for Your Goal

❁

1. Write a page on why you want your specific goal (it could be career- or relationship-related, whatever). Note down how fabulous your life will be when you achieve it and (very importantly) how much you deserve to be successful. Read this page whenever you lose your focus.

2. Visualize your successful outcome. See the detail, feel the emotions, be confident.

3. Write your action plan. Detail the steps you need to take and give yourself realistic deadlines for achieving them.

4. List your predicted obstacles and then list how you will overcome them. Be prepared.

5. Congratulate yourself each time you get closer to your goal.

Remember, you deserve success.

Lighten Up

❋

We are attracted to people who look on the lighter side of life. They don't bore us with their views on serious matters; they know how to let go of tensions and how to be flexible when things don't go their way.

When life is getting heavy and communication lines are closing, try lightening up the situation with humour and laughter. Let go of fixed ideas about how things 'should' be. Look at it all from a wider perspective – you will feel clearer and be more approachable.

Walk Yourself Clear

In this age of self-awareness there are
many therapies available for us to try.
One of the most powerful therapies is
free, is nearly always available and
doesn't hurt: the act of walking can
change our consciousness.

We can take our problems on a walk,
come home and things look different.

Walking is a type of meditation; it
makes our breathing rhythmic and as

our breathing expands and lifts, so does our mind.

When you feel like there's no space left inside your head, walk yourself clear. Just go! Do it! Let your inspiration return to you through your feet.

Accept Compliments Graciously

You have just met a friend in the street and she says, 'You are looking really great!' How do you respond? Here are some options:

1. Thanks.

2. Thanks, but I don't believe you.

3. Oh, no, I'm not! I've put on weight / got spots ...

Men are most likely to go for number 1 and women for variations on 2 and 3. Men don't indulge in false modesty but women are always inclined to belittle themselves. Step out of this social conditioning! The next time someone pays you a compliment just say 'Thanks' and believe it.

Stay Away from Complainers

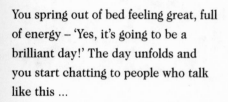

You spring out of bed feeling great, full of energy – 'Yes, it's going to be a brilliant day!' The day unfolds and you start chatting to people who talk like this ...

Oh no, I don't think you can do that ... Oh, this terrible weather, it makes me so depressed ... Isn't it awful about ...

and so it goes on until you might even start to feel guilty about feeling so good. Recognize what is happening, don't get sucked down into other people's negativity. Some people just love to burst a positive bubble, so stay away from them and protect your positive feelings.

Look at the Good News about You

It's time to stop letting negative thoughts get in your way. Never mind what you can't do; let's look at your assets.

Complete the following:

* My best asset is my ....
* I feel sexy when ....
* The thing I like best about my personality is ....

* The thing I like best about my body is ………
* The most incredible thing I have ever done is ………
* I feel attractive when ………
* I feel powerful when ………

Reflect on your answers. Think about your good news about yourself. You have a lot going for you.

Remember Girl, There's Always a Smile in your Pocket

❋

Our normal day-to-day existence can often feel so ordinary and mundane: getting up / looking after children / going to work / shopping / vacuuming the stairs / fetching or taking the children somewhere / watching TV / making dinner / putting out the rubbish ... When we are so routinized we can become bored, dissatisfied and miserable, and we take ourselves too seriously.

When you catch yourself in this mood, remember what my dear old grandad used to say: 'Girl, there's always a smile in your pocket'! That always made me laugh.

Lighten the load, put on that smile and feel the difference.

Enjoy the Unique Qualities of Others

Recognize that every human achievement demonstrates the incredible potential open to us all. But if we run a competitive race with others we will always lose. However hard we try, someone will always come along who will improve on our performance.

Learn from the achievements of

others and add this knowledge to your own experience. The human potential is incredible – we are so much more amazing than we think we are. Enjoy these possibilities instead of being defeated by them.

Make this powerful affirmation:

> *Everyone's success*
> *contributes to my success.*

Remember that we are all in this together!

Clear Your Clutter

❋

I have only been fascinated by house cleaning on three separate occasions in my life – a few hours before my children were born! Although I don't feel the same fascination for cleaning when I am not about to give birth, I do believe that cleaning and clearing out clutter are great forms of therapy whenever I am feeling stuck

somewhere in my life. When my mind
and heart aren't clear then the house
is a mess!

When you are feeling stuck, get to
grips with the clutter. Create a sense
of order in your environment and
your life will feel more ordered.

Show Your Appreciation

Feeling fed-up, miserable, bored, stuck or negative? Use this brilliant technique, make an appreciation list. Think of all the things that you appreciate in your life – your warm bed, the smell of roses, the taste of chocolate, the love of your child, the smile of a friend, your new coat. Write them all down, make a list as long as your arm (or longer).

* I (your name) ....
  appreciate ....

* I .... appreciate ....

* I .... appreciate ....

Your list of wonderful things will make
you smile and will lift your heart.

Appreciation is the key to happiness.

Let Go of Guilt

Guilt destroys self-esteem. Most women have a close relationship with guilt, living with such brain-teasers as:

'If I don't work we won't have enough money; if I do work I can't spend so much time with the children.'

Wracked with guilt we have been known to fly from pillar to post, trying to be all things to all people, always in a no-win situation, with our self-esteem falling as we go.

Whenever guilt attacks, just visualize it floating away in a bubble, never to be seen again. Don't think about it again, just let it go.

Don't Try to Be Perfect

It's just not good enough; it's not quite right; I'm not good enough; nothing I ever do is just right ... Are these statements familiar?

Nobody is perfect, we are always making mistakes. This is how we learn (yes, even us grown-ups).

The average child falls over 240 times before she learns to walk. No one expects her to walk immediately; she needs to practise. We are just grown-up little girls who also need to practise our skills, but while practising is fine, a continual quest for perfection can stop your creativity, your plans and projects. Enjoy what you do – it really is 'good enough' in itself.

Get Physical

✳

Escape from work, escape from the
house, escape from the family! Just
get out there and walk / run / cycle:
increase your feel-good endorphin
and oxygen levels, tone your muscles,
use up calories and come back feeling
great / more tolerant / happier / more
alert and productive.

Physical activity and a change of
scene can change your mood beyond

recognition. Take a brisk walk in your lunch break, cycle to school to pick up the children and walk them home, run around the park while the washing is drying. Get physically active and reap the feel-good rewards.

Focus on Your Strengths

Women seem to have a natural tendency to bring themselves down rather than to lift themselves up. Many of us have been taught that to be female is to be 'nice / pretty / quiet / submissive / receptive / thoughtful / kind / caring ...' Our brothers are more likely to have been encouraged to be outward-going, confident, goal-oriented and competitive.

Times are changing and women's life
expectations mirror that change. We
haven't concentrated on our strengths;
now it's time to do so. Focus on your
strengths. Make a (long) list of them.
Live them!

My strengths are:

* ....,...........

* ....

* ....

Do it Badly

❋

Just think of that beautiful painting,
marvellous novel or terrific film: the
people who made those things are so
talented and creative.

Have you ever wanted to embark on a
new project, only to stop yourself
because you know that you will fail to
be as brilliant as you want to be.

Remember that there are no overnight
sensations. Brilliant work comes from

one per cent inspiration and ninety-nine per cent dedication.
Perseverance is a part of this dedication and involves the creator (at some point) doing the painting / writing / acting / whatever ... badly.

Do it badly or don't do it at all!

Good work follows the bad.

Forgive Someone

Forgiveness is a powerful way of increasing our self-esteem. Forgiveness does not mean that we think it's OK for anybody to do anything to us. Forgiveness is all about letting go: if you cannot forgive someone, your angry thoughts will connect you to them forever.

Is there someone you find it difficult to forgive? If so, ask yourself what you gain from not forgiving this person.

1. Examine what hurt you and why.

2. Express this appropriately.

3. Forgive, let go and set yourself free!

How can you be high in self-esteem if you are trapped hating someone?

Look Beyond the Image

When you look in the mirror on a bad hair / skin / figure day the experience can really bring you down. Feeling not at your best can have an amazing impact on your whole day.

Look beyond your image and find something to admire about yourself – just one small thing will do to start.

Appreciate the colour of your eyes, the shape of your hands, your lovely smile. Keep appreciating some aspect of your appearance and your mood will lift; your confidence will increase and this will be reflected in the way you look.

Don't Bottle up
Your Anger

✳

The traditional view of women as the weaker sex, submissive, gentle and nurturing, has created generations of women who are uncomfortable with their own angry feelings. Anger is only an emotion, as valid and real as any other. Nevertheless, women will often suppress and deny their own anger, turning it inwards. This can lead to depression and eventually illness.

The next time you feel angry:

1. Recognize the feeling.

2. Work out why you are angry.

3. Find some immediate release (beating pillows, exercise, silent screaming).

4. Talk through your feelings with a friend.

5. If something needs to be said to someone, then say it!

Let Yourself Slow Down

Are you feeling rushed, pressurized and indecisive? Are you irritable and forgetful? These are all symptoms of belonging to the '24-hour society', in which we are able to buy anything and do anything at any time of day or night. This non-stop lifestyle places enormous pressure on us to keep going. It's getting harder than ever to know when or how to stop and relax.

Just slow down. Turn off the TV sometimes. Learn a relaxation technique. Leave your work at night. Create a real weekend (put the answermachine on). Protect your precious relaxation time.

Find a Group of Women

Women are different from men! Women in groups can offer each other such a wealth of emotional support, laughter, stress-release and physical support.

There are some aspects of our being that we can't or don't want to share with men. This is quite right and natural, so go out and join a class in aerobics, line dancing, yoga, pottery, massage, aromatherapy (or whatever appeals to you), for the benefit of the mutual female support you will find. There are lots of women attending all sorts of classes – go and find a group for yourself.

Women can empower themselves in relationships with other women.

Make a Date with Yourself

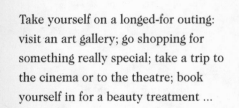

Take yourself on a longed-for outing:
visit an art gallery; go shopping for
something really special; take a trip to
the cinema or to the theatre; book
yourself in for a beauty treatment ...

Plan your date with yourself (when
you will go, what you will wear) just as
if you were going on a date with a
person who is very important to you.

Because you are going with an important person – yourself.

Don't go somewhere just because it's 'good' for you in some way. Choose something that you know you will enjoy. And don't stand yourself up (or let yourself down).

Be your own best friend – always!

Heal Your Life

Make any of these affirmations as
often as you can. Write them, say
them, sing them. Surround yourself
with healing consciousness and feel
your energy respond.

I deserve vibrant health.

I love my body.

I can heal myself.

I listen and respond to my body's
    messages.

I create harmony and balance
  within my body.

The universal life-force flows easily
  through me.

I trust my inner messages.

It is safe to be well.

I am ready to be well, now.

I love and value myself.

Accept Your Aloneness

Sometimes our aloneness may be very scary. We may feel lonely: that no one can ever really understand how we feel or always 'be there' for us.

It's true, no one will ever know the inner you. You are the only person who can know yourself. And would you really want anyone to know everything about you?

Accept your aloneness and you will be free to be yourself: you can release your expectations of people to know all about you and you can stop feeling guilty about not always being able to 'be there' for others.

Congratulate
Yourself

※

Congratulate yourself for recognizing
your power to change the quality of
your life. Increase your Woman Power
and your life will be transformed,
which in turn will change the lives of
everyone you meet.

Woman Power is your birthright but
you have to work for it. This work is
not always easy. Sometimes it feels

impossible to believe in yourself, but never doubt your progress, even when darkness surrounds you. Know that all the love and support you need will always be with you. The darkest hour is truly just before the dawn and you will come shining through!

About the Author

Lynda Field is a trained counsellor and psychotherapist specializing in personal and group development.

Visit Lynda online at www.lyndafield.com

Her other books include the best-selling

Creating Self-Esteem

The Self-Esteem Workbook

Self-Esteem for Women

And 60 Tips for Self-Esteem.

She lives in Essex, England.

Lynda Field Books also available from
Vermilion

60 Ways to Change Your Life   £2.50

60 Ways to Feel Amazing   £2.50

To order copies of any of these books
direct from Vermilion call TBS Direct
credit card hotline on 01206 255800

Vermilion books are also available from
all good booksellers.